'Il vero lusso di una mensa sta nel dessert'
The real luxury of a meal lies in the dessert.
From *Il Piacere* by Gabriele D'Annunzio

ANNA DEL CONTE'S ITALIAN KITCHEN
I DOLCI

ILLUSTRATED BY FLO BAYLEY

PAVILION

First published in Great Britain in 1993 by
PAVILION BOOKS LIMITED
26 Upper Ground, London SE1 9PD

Copyright © Anna Del Conte 1993
Illustrations copyright © Flo Bayley 1993

The moral right of the author has been asserted

Designed by Andrew Barron & Collis Clements Associates

A CIP catalogue record for this book is available from the British Library

ISBN 1 85793 0436

Printed and bound in Italy by New Interlitho

2 4 6 8 10 9 7 5 3 1

This book may be ordered by post direct from the publisher. Please contact
the Marketing Department. But try your bookshop first.

CONTENTS

DOLCI

Italians love sweets, although they only eat them on special occasions. An everyday meal ends with fresh fruit; sweets are kept for Sundays, parties, family gatherings, religious days and village *feste*.

Dolci developed differently in northern, central and southern Italy. The dolci of the north are often little more than sweet breads, the panettone milanese being the prime example. The dolci of central Italy are richer, with lots of spices, nuts, candied peel and honey, as in the panforte from Siena or the *certosino* from Bologna. It was also in this part of the country that there originated the '*dolci al cucchiaio*' (sweets that can be eaten with a spoon such as the *zuppe inglesi*, or trifles) of Emilia-Romagna and Tuscany. In southern Italy the protagonists of dolci are almonds and candied fruits, a heritage from Arab cooking. And it is here that dolci reach the highest level of culinary art.

This being Italy, there are, of course, many exceptions to this rule. After all, the birthplace of zabaglione – the *dolce al cucchiaio* par excellence – is Piedmont in the north, while a *ciambella* – sweet ring-shaped bread made with potatoes, eggs and flour – is a traditional dolce of Apulia.

As they are eaten on feast days, dolci are even more regional than other kinds of food. Every patron saint, every feast day of the year, has its own special dolce, in every town in Italy. The region that has more special occasions, and more legends, associated with its dolci is Sicily. There are biscuits called *frutti di morte* – fruits of death – made with *pasta reale* – almond paste – that are eaten at the end of a meal on All Soul's day, 2 November. The *sfinci di San Giuseppe* are a sort of fritter eaten on St Joseph's day, 19 March. For Easter Sunday a magnificent *agnello pasquale* – Easter lamb – is made in Sicily with a pastry, strongly flavoured with cloves, that is moulded in the shape of a lamb.

Some of these special dolci have become so popular that they are now eaten all year round, not only in Italy but abroad, as is the case with panettone and panforte, both originally eaten only at Christmas. Others are still very localised and known only in the place where they are made. When I was in Sicily recently I ate some superb soft biscuits called *olivette di Sant'Agata*. They were made of marzipan, sugar, rum and vanilla, and are a speciality of Catania, made originally on the saint's day of Sant'Agata, a local martyr. I had never heard of *olivette* before, yet they are the best almond-based sweets I have ever had. Our Sicilian hostess insisted that we drive many, many miles along the motorway to an old fashioned *pasticceria* in Catania to buy 'the only *olivette* worth eating'. The lengths Italians will go in their search for excellence, as far as food is concerned, never ceases to amaze me.

The tradition of excellence in Italian dolci goes back a long way. Writing in Naples at the beginning of the nineteenth century, Lady Blessington, a friend of Emma Hamilton, commented, 'Italian confectionery and ices are far superior to those of the French and the English, and their variety is infinite.' A passage from *Il Gattopardo* by Giuseppe Tomasi di Lampedusa gives a good idea of what Lady Blessington meant. He describes how, at the great ball, the table was covered with pink parfaits, champagne parfaits, grey parfaits which parted creaking under the blade of the cake knife; a violin melody in major of candied morello cherries; acid notes of yellow pineapples; and the *trionfi della gola* – triumphs of gluttony – with the opaque green of their pistachio paste, and the shameless *minni di virgini* – virgins' breasts.'

Note: all spoon measures should be level.

TORTE E CROSTATE

CAKES AND TARTS

The emphasis of this section is on cakes containing fruit and nuts.

In Italy, cakes, even the drier sort, are often eaten as part of a meal. Cakes are also served mid-morning or after supper, when they are traditionally accompanied by a glass of wine. Wine, after all, used to be the cheapest beverage, one that even poor people in the country could afford. They made their own wine, while tea or coffee had to be bought.

The section ends with two recipes for tarts. Tarts are not as common in Italy as in France, but the ones I have chosen are very characteristic and, so far as I know, are only to be found in their place of origin.

In all the cake and biscuit recipes, I recommend the use of Italian 00 flour. This is a high-quality flour with very little flavour and very good raising properties. It is available from specialist Italian shops.

TORTA DI PERE E BANANE
PEAR AND BANANA PIE

Serves 8

1 unwaxed lemon
2 large, ripe but firm, good
quality pears, about 450g/1lb
2 large bananas
unsalted butter for the tin
2 tbsp plain flour
1½ tbsp caster sugar

For the pastry

250g/9oz plain flour, preferably
Italian 00 (see page 7)
1 tsp baking powder
½ tsp salt
100g/3½oz caster sugar
120g/4oz unsalted butter, cut
into small pieces
1 egg yolk
2–4 tbsp milk

Some Italian pies and tarts are made with a pastry that is quite soft, halfway between a short pastry and a sponge. This is because baking powder is added to the pastry mixture. It is particularly suitable for pies, when it envelops a moist filling, as in this recipe.

1 Scrub and dry the lemon, then grate the zest. Squeeze the juice.
2 To make the pastry dough, sift the flour with the baking powder and salt on to a work surface. Mix in half the grated lemon zest and the sugar, then rub in the butter. Add the egg yolk and enough milk to bind to a dough. (You can make the pastry dough in a food processor, but be careful when you add the milk.) Form a ball, wrap and chill for at least 2 hours.
3 Peel the pears. Cut into quarters, remove cores and then cut into chunks. Put in a bowl and add the lemon juice and the remaining zest.
4 Peel the bananas and cut into slices. Add to the pears and mix well. Leave to macerate for about 30 minutes.
5 Heat the oven to 180°C/350°F/Gas Mark 4.
6 Lightly butter a 22.5cm/9in loose-based flan tin.
7 Mix the flour with the sugar.
8 Cut off about two-thirds of the dough and roll it out into a circle large enough to cover the bottom and sides of the tin. Press gently into the tin. Sprinkle two-thirds of the flour and sugar mixture over the dough. With a slotted spoon, transfer the fruit to the tin, leaving the juices behind in the bowl. Sprinkle the remaining flour and sugar mixture over the fruit.
9 Roll out the rest of the dough to cover the pie and place over the fruit. Seal the edge, pressing down with the prongs of a fork.

Make a few holes on the surface with the fork for the steam to escape.

10 Place the tin in the oven. Bake for 50–60 minutes or until the pastry is golden.

11 Allow to cool in the tin and then carefully unmould and transfer to a flat dish.

If you are serving the pie at the end of a meal, a bowl of whipped cream goes well with it.

TORTA DI MELE

APPLE CAKE

When I was in Italy recently, I asked my cousin Mariella for a recipe for an apple cake. All my cousins are good cooks, and some of my recipes come from them. Back home, a few months later, I found no less than five recipes for Mariella's apple cakes. Very disturbing. But only one was marked '*Buonissima*', so I began with this one and have never bothered with the others.

It certainly is very good, with its homely appearance yet rich buttery base, which is covered with a thick layer of very thin slices of lemon-flavoured apples. This type of cake is not served with cream in Italy, not for health reasons, but because it is better without.

1 Peel the apples. Cut into quarters, remove the core and slice thinly. Put the slices in a bowl. Add the lemon juice and mix the apple slices so that they all share the juice. Leave to macerate while you prepare the cake mixture.

2 Beat the egg yolks with the caster sugar until pale and mousse-like. Add the butter and stir until totally incorporated.

Serves 8

900g/2lb good dessert apples
juice of 1 lemon
2 size-2 eggs, separated
150g/5oz caster sugar
120g/4oz unsalted butter, melted
150g/5oz plain flour, preferably Italian 00 (see page 7)
1 tbsp baking powder
$\frac{1}{2}$ tsp salt
unsalted butter and dried breadcrumbs for the tin

To finish
30g/1oz unsalted butter, melted
icing sugar

3 Heat the oven to 180°C/350°F/Gas Mark 4.

4 Sift together the flour, baking powder and salt.

5 Whisk the egg whites until stiff but not dry. Sprinkle 2 tbsp of the flour mixture over the egg mixture and fold it in with 2 tbsp of the whisked egg whites. Repeat this addition of flour and egg white, folding them in very gently with a high movement.

6 Butter a 25cm/10in spring-clip cake tin and sprinkle with breadcrumbs to coat the bottom and sides. Throw away excess crumbs. Spoon the cake mixture into the tin and cover with layers of sliced apple.

7 Pour the melted butter all over the apple slices and place the tin in the oven. This cake takes at least 1 hour to bake. If it is browning too much at the edge, turn the heat down a little and continue baking until the middle is cooked. Test by inserting a wooden cocktail stick; it should come out dry.

8 Turn the tin over on to a wire rack, remove the clip band and the base of the tin, and allow the cake to cool. When cold, turn the cake over on to a flat round serving dish and sprinkle lavishly with sifted icing sugar. Do this just before serving or the sugar will soak into the cake and disappear.

TORTA DI CIOCCOLATO FARCITA DI ZABAIONE

CHOCOLATE AND ZABAGLIONE CAKE

Serves 8

60g/2oz bitter chocolate
100g/3½oz unsalted butter, at room temperature
180g/6oz caster sugar
3 size-2 eggs, at room temperature, separated
1½ tbsp dark rum
100g/3½oz plain flour, preferably Italian 00 (see page 7)
100g/3½oz potato flour
1½ tsp baking powder
½ tsp salt
1 tsp lemon juice
unsalted butter and flour for the tin
150ml/¼pt double cream

For the zabaglione

4 size-2 egg yolks
5 tbsp caster sugar
a piece of vanilla pod
120ml/4 fl oz dry Marsala or medium sherry

My editor, Gillian Young, sampled this cake when she came to tea the other day, and declared it very well worth writing about. This endorsed my opinion, because it has the perfect balance of chocolate, sugar and alcohol. The zabaglione, poured on each half of the cake, partly sinks into the sponge. This makes a thin layer in the middle of the cake, giving it two slightly different textures.

Like many Italian cooks, I often replace half the plain flour with the same amount of potato flour for more lightness in the sponge; it is these quantities which are given below.

1 Heat the oven to 130°C/250°F/Gas Mark ½. Break the chocolate into small pieces, put in a heatproof bowl and warm in the oven until the chocolate has melted. Set the chocolate aside. Turn the oven heat up to 190°C/375°F/Gas Mark 5.
2 Beat the butter until it is soft. Add the sugar and beat together until pale and creamy. Gradually beat in the egg yolks, rum and melted chocolate.
3 Sift the two flours, baking powder and salt through a fine sieve twice.
4 Whisk the egg whites with the lemon juice until stiff but not dry. (The lemon juice, being acid, helps to stabilise the froth without increasing its volume.)
5 Add 1 tbsp of the flour mixture and 1 tbsp of the egg white and fold into the chocolate mixture with a high movement, using a metal spoon. Continue adding alternate spoonfuls of flour mixture and egg white.

6 Generously butter a 20cm/8in spring-clip cake tin. Sprinkle with flour, then shake out excess flour. Spoon the cake mixture into the tin and place in the oven. The cake will be cooked in about 45 minutes. To see if it is ready, insert a wooden cocktail stick into the middle; it should come out dry.

7 Leave the cake in the tin for about 10 minutes to settle and then turn it out on to a wire rack to cool.

8 Meanwhile, make the zabaglione. Put the egg yolks, sugar and vanilla in a round-bottomed metal bowl or in the upper part of a double boiler. Beat well with a small balloon whisk. Beat in the Marsala. Set the bowl in a bain-marie, i.e. in a pan containing simmering water, or set the double boiler pan over the bottom pan. Continue beating until the mixture is dense and thick.

9 Cut the cake horizontally in half. Make some slits in the cut face of each half and pour about two-thirds of the zabaglione all over them. Do this slowly to allow the zabaglione to penetrate into the sponge. Put the two halves together again. Refrigerate for at least 6 hours.

10 Whip the cream until stiff. Whisk the rest of the zabaglione until it is thick again, then mix evenly with the cream. Cover the top of the cake with this mixture. Keep the cake in the fridge until you want to serve it.

TORTA DI CIOCCOLATO CON LE PERE
CHOCOLATE AND PEAR CAKE

Serves 4–6

75g/2½oz bitter chocolate, broken into small pieces
75g/2½oz unsalted butter, at room temperature
75g/2½oz icing sugar, sifted
1 egg, at room temperature, separated
2 egg yolks, at room temperature
pinch of ground cinnamon
pinch of salt
120g/4oz plain flour, preferably Italian 00 (see page 7)
1 large, ripe but firm William's pear, about 225g/½lb
unsalted butter and flour for the tin
icing sugar, to decorate

I make this cake in a loaf tin, as it used to be made at home for our *merenda* – afternoon tea. If you want to serve it as a dessert, I suggest making it in a 15cm/6in round tin.

1 Heat the oven to 130°C/250°F/Gas Mark ½. Put the chocolate in a heatproof bowl and melt it in the oven. Remove from the oven and keep in a warm place. Turn the oven heat up to 180°C/350°F/Gas Mark 4.

2 Beat the butter until really soft. I use a hand-held electric mixer. Gradually add the icing sugar while beating constantly, then beat until light and pale yellow. (If you add all the sugar at once and start beating butter and sugar together, you will find the sugar flying everywhere except in the butter.) Add the 3 egg yolks, cinnamon, salt and melted chocolate.

3 Whisk the egg white until stiff but not dry and then fold it into the mixture by the spoonful, alternating it with spoonfuls of flour. Fold lightly but thoroughly.

4 Peel and core the pear and cut it into 1cm/½in cubes. Mix lightly into the mixture.

5 Butter a loaf tin that is approximately 17.5 × 10 × 5cm/7 × 4 × 2in. Sprinkle in 1 tbsp of flour, shake the tin so the flour covers all the surface and then throw away the excess flour. Spoon the cake mixture into the tin. Bake for about 50 minutes or until the sides of the cake have shrunk from the tin and the cake is dry in the middle – test by inserting a wooden cocktail stick.

6 Remove the tin from the oven, unmould the cake on to a wire rack and leave to cool.

7 Sprinkle with sifted icing sugar just before serving.

TORTA DI NOCI
WALNUT CAKE

Serves 6–8

120g/4oz unsalted butter, at
room temperature
180g/6oz icing sugar, sifted
3 size-2 eggs, at room
temperature, separated
150g/5oz walnut pieces
120g/4oz plain flour, preferably
Italian 00 (see page 7)
$\frac{1}{2}$ tbsp baking powder
pinch of salt
grated zest of 1 unwaxed lemon
$\frac{1}{4}$ tsp lemon juice
unsalted butter and dried
breadcrumbs for the tin
icing sugar, to decorate

Buy your walnuts from a shop with a quick turnover so that they will not be old and rancid. Better still, buy the nuts in their shells at Christmas time and shell them yourself. Keep them in the freezer.

1 Heat the oven to 180°C/350°F/Gas Mark 4.

2 Beat the butter until very soft. Gradually beat in the icing sugar to make a smooth thick cream. Use a hand-held electric mixer, if you have one.

3 Lightly beat the egg yolks together with a fork, then add gradually to the butter cream, mixing thoroughly to incorporate.

4 Put the walnuts in a food processor and process until very coarsely ground while pulsing the machine. The nuts should be grainy, not ground fine. Stir into the butter mixture.

5 Sift the flour, baking powder and salt together and fold into the butter mixture with the lemon zest.

6 Whisk the egg whites with the lemon juice until stiff but not dry and fold into the mixture, using a metal spoon and lifting it high to incorporate more air.

7 Generously butter a 20cm/8in spring-clip cake tin. Sprinkle with breadcrumbs, shake the tin to cover all the surface and then shake out excess crumbs. Spoon the cake mixture into the prepared tin.

8 Bake in the preheated oven for about 45 minutes or until the cake is done. Test by inserting a wooden cocktail stick into the middle of the cake; it should come out dry. Unclip the side band and turn the cake over on to a wire rack to cool.

9 Sprinkle lavishly with sifted icing sugar before serving.

TORTA DI RICOTTA
RICOTTA CAKE

I do believe that some of the best recipes come from family *ricettari* – recipe collections. These are recipes for dishes that are suited to home cooking, and have been tested and improved over the years by generations of cooks. This is such a one.

Serves 10–12

120g/4oz sultanas
300g/10oz caster sugar
120g/4oz unsalted butter, at room temperature
4 size-2 eggs, at room temperature
grated zest of 1 unwaxed lemon
6 tbsp potato flour
1 tbsp baking powder
$\frac{1}{2}$ tsp salt
1kg/2$\frac{1}{4}$lb fresh ricotta
unsalted butter for the tin
icing sugar, to decorate

1 Soak the sultanas in hot water for 15 minutes to puff them up.
2 Reserve 1 tbsp of the caster sugar. Beat the butter with the remaining caster sugar until pale and creamy and then add the eggs, one at a time. When all the eggs have been incorporated, mix in the lemon zest, potato flour, baking powder and salt.
3 Heat the oven to 180°C/350°F/Gas Mark 4.
4 Press the ricotta through the small-hole disc of a food mill, or through a sieve, directly on to the other ingredients. Do not use a food processor as this would not aereate the ricotta. Fold the ricotta thoroughly into the mixture. Drain the sultanas, pat them dry with kitchen paper towels and fold into the mixture.
5 Generously butter a 25cm/10in spring-clip cake tin and sprinkle with the reserved caster sugar to coat the bottom and sides.
6 Spoon the ricotta mixture into the tin and bake for 1–1$\frac{1}{4}$ hours or until the cake is done (it will shrink slightly from the sides of the tin). Leave to cool in the tin. Unmould the cake when cold and place on a flat serving dish. Sprinkle with plenty of sifted icing sugar just before serving.

LA TORTA SBRISOLONA

CRUMBLY CAKE

Serves 6

120g/4oz almonds
120g/4oz granulated sugar
150g/5oz plain flour
120g/4oz coarse cornmeal
grated zest of 1 unwaxed lemon
pinch of salt
2 egg yolks
120g/4oz unsalted butter, at
room temperature
unsalted butter for the tin
icing sugar, to decorate

The word *sbrisolona* is derived from *briciola* (stress on the first syllable), meaning 'crumb', which is what this cake seems to consist of. If you want it less crumbly, you can cut it into slices with a sharp knife when it is still hot. But I find that part of its appeal is its rustic appearance, as well, of course, as its deliciousness. My husband's comment on it, as he munched, was, 'This cake is not just moreish; once you start eating it, you can't stop.'

It is an ideal cake to take with tea or coffee in the afternoon, or with sweet wine at any time of day.

1 Heat the oven to 200°C/400°F/Gas Mark 6.

2 Drop the almonds into a pan of boiling water and boil for 30 seconds after the water has come back to the boil. Drain and remove the skin by squeezing the almonds between your fingers. Spread them on a baking tray and toast them in the oven for 7 minutes or until golden brown. Turn the heat down to 180°C/350°F/Gas Mark 4.

3 Put the almonds in a food processor with 2 tbsp of the granulated sugar and process until they are reduced to a coarse powder.

4 In a bowl, mix the flour, cornmeal, the remaining granulated sugar, lemon zest, ground almonds and salt. Add the egg yolks and work with your hands until the mixture is crumbly.

5 Add the butter to the crumbly mixture and work again to incorporate it thoroughly, until the dough sticks together in crumbly mass.

6 Generously butter a 20cm/8in shallow round cake tin and line the bottom with siliconised baking parchment. Spread the mixture evenly in the tin, pressing it down with your hands. Bake for 40–45 minutes or until the cake is golden brown and a skewer inserted in the centre comes out dry.

7 Turn out the cake on to a wire rack and peel off the baking parchment. Leave to cool. Before serving, sprinkle the cake with sifted icing sugar.

This cake keeps very well for several days.

PANFORTE

Serves 8–10

60g/2oz candied fruit
60/2oz preserved ginger
150g/5oz mixed candied
orange, lemon and citron peel
60g/2oz ground hazelnuts
100g/3½oz whole hazelnuts
100g/3½oz almonds
60g/2oz walnut pieces
1 tsp ground cinnamon
large pinch of freshly grated
nutmeg
large pinch of ground cloves
large pinch of freshly ground
white pepper
large pinch of ground ginger
large pinch of ground coriander
4 tbsp plain flour
1 tbsp cocoa powder
4 tbsp granulated sugar
4 tbsp clear honey
oil and rice paper for the tin
1 tbsp icing sugar

Panforte is one of the most ancient dolci. A reference to 'a spicy and honeyed bread' brought back to Siena from the Middle East appears in Dante's *Inferno*. It is the traditional Christmas cake of Siena, but is now available all the year round.

There are two kinds of panforte, a white panforte and a black one. The white is the older version. The black was created when cocoa arrived from the New World and became the fashionable ingredient.

My recipe contains a little cocoa and makes a softer panforte than the commercial one. I have also substituted preserved ginger for candied pumpkin, which is not available in this country. The ginger is an excellent substitute, both for its flavour and by being in keeping with the early origins of panforte, when spices, just arrived from the Orient, were used very prodigally as a show of wealth.

1 Heat the oven to 180°C/350°F/Gas Mark 4.
2 Coarsely chop all the candied fruit and peel and place in a bowl. (This can be done in a food processor: cut the candied fruits and peel into pieces, put in the food processor and process for a short time, while shaking the machine backwards and forwards. Do not reduce to a paste.)
3 Spread the ground hazelnuts and the whole hazelnuts on two baking trays. Toast the ground hazelnuts in the oven for about 5 minutes and the whole hazelnuts for 10 minutes. Shake the trays gently from time to time. Add the ground hazelnuts to the candied fruits in the bowl.
4 Allow the whole hazelnuts to cool slightly and then rub them, a few at a time, in a coarse towel to remove the skin. Place the

nuts in a coarse sieve and shake to separate the skin from the nuts. Chop the nuts coarsely and add to the bowl.

5 Chop the almonds and walnuts coarsely and add to the bowl.

6 Put aside $\frac{1}{2}$ tsp of the cinnamon. Sift the rest of the cinnamon, all the other spices, the flour and cocoa powder directly into the bowl. Mix well.

7 Put the granulated sugar and honey into a small saucepan. Cook over low heat until the sugar has completely dissolved. Add to the bowl and mix very well with your hands.

8 Line the bottom of a 17.5cm/7in loose-based flan tin with rice paper and grease the sides of the tin with oil. Press the mixture evenly into the tin. Leave to stand at room temperature for 5 hours or longer if possible.

9 Preheat the oven to 170°C/325°F/Gas Mark 3.

10 Put the remaining cinnamon and the icing sugar in a sieve and sprinkle over the top of the cake. Bake for about 50 minutes.

11 Remove from the oven and leave to cool for 10 minutes, then remove the panforte from the tin and cool completely on a wire rack. When cold, wrap in foil and store.

Panforte will keep for at least 2–3 months.

PASTIERA NAPOLETANA

NEAPOLITAN TART

Serves 8–10

250g/9oz dried whole wheat, to be soaked, or 400g/14oz canned cooked wheat
600ml/1pt full fat milk
pinch of salt
grated zest of ½ lemon and ½ orange
piece of vanilla pod, about 5cm/2in long, or a few drops of vanilla essence
½ tsp ground cinnamon
300g/10oz fresh ricotta
4 eggs, at room temperature, separated
2 egg yolks
225g/8oz caster sugar
2 tbsp orange flower water
120g/4oz candied peel, cut into tiny pieces
unsalted butter for the tin
icing sugar, to decorate

For the pastry
300g/10oz plain flour, preferably Italian 00 (see page 7)
6 tbsp icing sugar
pinch of salt
grated zest of ½ unwaxed lemon
150g/5oz unsalted butter, cut into small pieces
3 size-2 egg yolks

At Easter time, bakers and *pasticceri* in Naples compete with each other to produce the best *pastiere*, the beloved tart of the Neapolitans, made with whole wheat and ricotta. You can now buy whole wheat in cans, called Gran Pastiera, in Italian shops. It is good, and saves the long labour of soaking the grain.

1 If you are using dried whole wheat, soak the grains in cold water for 48 hours. Rinse and drain them.
2 Put the soaked wheat in a saucepan with the milk, salt, lemon and orange zest, the vanilla pod and cinnamon and bring to the boil. Simmer over the lowest possible heat for 3–4 hours or until the grain is cooked and tender. Leave it to cool for at least 8 hours (24 hours is better) to allow the grain to swell. Remove and discard the vanilla pod.
3 If you are using canned wheat, just add the lemon and orange zest, vanilla essence and cinnamon.

4 Make the pastry dough: sift the flour, sugar and salt onto a work surface. Mix in the lemon zest, then rub in the butter. Add the egg yolks and knead together briefly to make a smooth and compact dough. (The dough can also be made in a food processor.) Wrap and chill for at least 2 hours.

5 To make the filling, beat the ricotta with the 6 egg yolks. Add the caster sugar, orange flower water, candied peel and grain mixture. Mix very thoroughly.

6 Whisk the 4 egg whites until stiff but not dry. Fold into the grain and ricotta mixture lightly but thoroughly.

7 Heat the oven to 180°C/350°F/Gas Mark 4. Butter a 25cm/10in spring-clip cake tin. Roll out about two-thirds of the pastry dough and press into the tin, making sure it is of the same thickness all over the bottom and up the sides. Spoon in the filling.

8 Roll out the remaining dough and cut into long strips. Place the strips over the filling to form a lattice top. Bake for 45–50 minutes or until the filling is set and the pastry is golden brown. Allow to cool and then turn out. Dust with sifted icing sugar before serving.

LA CROSTATA DI BIETOLE
SWISS CHARD AND CRÈME
PÂTISSIÈRE TART

Serves 6

450g/1lb Swiss chard
3 tbsp granulated sugar
5 cloves
2 tbsp sultanas
2 tbsp pine nuts
20g/⅔oz bitter chocolate, cut
into small pieces
icing sugar, to decorate

For the pastry
225g/8oz plain flour, preferably
Italian 00 (see page 7)
60g/2oz caster sugar
2 pinches of salt
90g/3oz unsalted butter, cut
into small pieces
2 egg yolks
2 tbsp hot milk

For the crème pâtissière
300ml/½pt full-fat milk
pared strip of unwaxed
lemon zest
pared strip of unwaxed
orange zest
1 cinnamon stick
piece of vanilla pod
2 egg yolks
50g/1¾oz caster sugar
2 tbsp plain flour

I had this extraordinary tart at the San Martino restaurant in London. I find it extraordinary because of the use of Swiss chard in a sweet dish, something I had never met before. Yet the owner of the San Martino assured me that in his native province of Lucca the tart is called 'La Torta della Nonna' – grandmother's tart, a name that proves its popularity.

It is quite delicious, as well as being mysterious in its remote chocolatey taste.

1 To make the pastry dough, pile the flour on the work surface, mix in the sugar and salt and rub in the butter. Add the egg yolks and hot milk and work quickly to a smooth dough. Form a ball, wrap and chill for at least 2 hours.
2 Roll out two-thirds of the dough into a circle 5mm/¼in thick. Line a 17.5cm/7in loose-based flan tin with the circle of dough, pressing firmly into the corners. Put back into the fridge while you prepare the filling.
3 To make the crème pâtissière, put the milk in a saucepan, add all the flavourings and bring to the boil. Draw off the heat and leave to infuse for about 1 hour.
4 Put the egg yolks and sugar into a heavy-bottomed saucepan and beat until the eggs are pale yellow and creamy. Add the flour gradually.
5 Strain the milk and return to its pan. Bring back to simmering point. Off the heat, add very gradually to the egg and flour mixture, beating constantly.
6 Put the saucepan over low heat and bring to a simmer, while stirring constantly. Simmer for 5 minutes to cook the flour and

then draw off the heat. Place the base of the pan in a sink of cold water to cool quickly.

7 Remove the Swiss chard stalks from the leaves; reserve the stalks for another dish. Bring 300ml/$\frac{1}{2}$pt of water to the boil. Add the granulated sugar and cloves and stir to dissolve the sugar. Plunge in the Swiss chard leaves, stir well and cook until tender. Drain, but do not squeeze the liquid out. Set aside.

8 Heat the oven to 200°C/400°F/Gas Mark 6.

9 Spread a little of the crème pâtissière over the bottom of the pastry case. Cover with about half the Swiss chard and sprinkle with half the sultanas, pine nuts and chocolate pieces. Spread on another layer of crème, then more Swiss chard and finally the remaining crème. Sprinkle the remaining sultanas, pine nuts and chocolate pieces over the top.

10 Roll out the remaining pastry. Cut 6 strips, each about 1 cm/$\frac{1}{2}$in wide, and lay them on top of the tart in a criss-cross fashion to form a lattice. Bake for 20 minutes or until the pastry is golden brown. Allow to cool in the tin. When cold, turn out and sprinkle the top with sifted icing sugar.

BISCOTTI E FRITTELLE

─ BISCUITS AND FRITTERS ─

If you open a regional Italian cookery book, you will find more recipes for biscuits than for any other type of sweet. This is because, in Italy, sweets tend to be eaten at any time of day, whereas to have a pudding at the end of a meal is unusual. Biscuits are often eaten casually, as a snack, with a glass of wine, sitting round the kitchen table.

From the vast range of sweet fritters in Italy I have picked two recipes which I particularly like. Fritters are amongst the most ancient of foods; in Roman times they were prepared and eaten in the streets on pagan feast days, just as they are today at village feasts. Frying, after all, is the most immediate of cooking methods, and requires only a saucepan full of oil.

In all the cake and biscuit recipes, I recommend the use of Italian 00 flour. This is a high-quality flour with very little flavour and very good raising properties. it is available from specialist Italian shops.

BACI DI DAMA

LADY'S KISSES

Makes about 35 biscuits

120g/4oz best almonds
120g/4oz caster sugar
120g/4oz unsalted butter, at
room temperature
1 tsp pure vanilla essence
pinch of salt
120g/4oz plain flour, preferably
Italian 00 (see page 27)
unsalted butter for the trays
100g/3½oz bitter chocolate

The name of these biscuits is just as lovely as the biscuits themselves. They are a speciality of Tortona, a town in southern Piedmont.

1 Heat the oven to 180°C/350°F/Gas Mark 4.

2 Blanch the almonds in boiling water for 30 seconds. Drain and squeeze them in your fingers to remove the skins. Spread them on a baking tray and put in the oven for 5 minutes to dry thoroughly.

3 Put the almonds in a food processor. Add 1–2 tbsp of the sugar (this absorbs the oil from the nuts) and process to a fine powder. Add the butter, vanilla and salt and process again until the mixture is very creamy. Transfer to a bowl.

4 Sift the flour into the bowl. Fold in the flour very thoroughly to make a dough.

5 Break off pieces of the dough, the size of cherries, and roll them into balls between the palms of your hands. Place them on buttered baking trays, spacing them about 2cm/¾in apart. Bake for about 15 minutes or until golden brown. Leave to cool on the trays for about 5 minutes and then transfer to a wire rack to cool completely.

6 Melt the chocolate in a bain-marie. When the biscuits are cold, spread a little of the chocolate over one biscuit and make a sandwich by sticking another biscuit to the chocolate.

I BISCOTTI DELLA NONNA CATERINA

MY GRANDMOTHER'S BISCUITS

There is an infinite number of 'Torte della Nonna', but unfortunately none I can claim for <u>my</u> grandmother. However, she made these lovely biscuits that are ideal for serving with ice-creams or mousses, or to have with coffee.

1 Heat the oven to 180°C/350°F/Gas Mark 4.

2 Beat the egg yolks with the rum. Add the sugar and beat hard until pale.

3 Sift the flour with the salt and add gradually to the egg and sugar mixture, stirring hard the whole time.

4 Add the butter and beat until the mixture is well blended.

5 Butter two baking trays. To form the biscuits, dampen your hands, pick up a little dollop of the biscuit dough and shape it into a round. Place the rounds on the trays, leaving about 5cm/2in between each one, because the mixture spreads out a lot while cooking. Bake for 15–20 minutes or until deep gold.

6 Remove the trays from the oven and transfer the biscuits to a wire rack to cool.

These biscuits will keep well for a week in an airtight tin.

Makes about 24 biscuits

2 size-2 egg yolks
2 tbsp rum
120g/4oz caster sugar
150g/5oz plain flour, preferably Italian 00 (see page 27)
pinch of salt
100g/3½oz unsalted butter, very soft but not melted
butter and flour for the trays

LE BISSE

S-SHAPED BISCUITS

Makes about 40 biscuits

3 eggs
180g/6oz caster sugar
150ml/¼pt vegetable or olive oil
grated zest of 1 unwaxed lemon
500g/1lb 2oz plain flour,
preferably Italian 00 (see
page 27)
pinch of salt
oil for baking trays

A *bissa* is a water snake in Venetian dialect, which explains the name of these little biscuits. They are to be found in any bakery or *pasticceria* in Venice, but they can easily be made at home. Use an oil without flavour.

1 In a large bowl, whisk the eggs with the sugar until pale and frothy. Add the oil and lemon zest, then fold in the flour and salt. Knead well. Wrap the dough and chill it for about 1 hour.
2 Preheat the oven to 220°C/425°F/Gas Mark 7.
3 Grease 2 large baking trays with a little oil.
4 To shape each biscuit, take a little ball of dough and roll it into a sausage shape a little more than 1cm/½in thick and 12.5cm/5in long. Curve into the form of an 'S' and set on a baking tray.
5 Bake for 5 minutes, then reduce the heat to 180°C/350°F/Gas Mark 4 and bake for a further 10–15 minutes or until pale golden. Cool slightly on the baking trays before transferring to a wire rack to cool completely.

CROSTOLI TRENTINI
FRITTERS FROM NORTHERN ITALY

At Carnival time, every bakery or *pasticceria* in northern and central Italy makes a show of huge trays piled high with puffy golden fritters sprinkled with icing sugar. They are the traditional Carnival fare, made in different shapes in various regions. Thus there are *cenci*, meaning rags, in Tuscany, *chiacchiere*, chatterings, in Lombardy, *galani*, ribbons, in Venice and *sfrappole* in Emilia. The dough varies only a little. What changes is the shape.

The original crostoli from Trentino and Friuli are strips of dough tied together in a loose knot, but they are often cut, as in my recipe, which is easier and quicker. If you serve them at the end of a meal, hand round a bowl of whipped cream to dollop over the crostoli.

Serves 6

150g/5oz plain flour, preferably
Italian 00 (see page 27)
1½ tbsp caster sugar
½ tsp baking powder
pinch of salt
30g/1 oz unsalted butter, at
room temperature
1 size-2 egg yolk
3 tbsp grappa (Italian eau-de-vie)
or white rum
1–2 tbsp semi-skimmed milk
oil for frying
icing sugar, to decorate

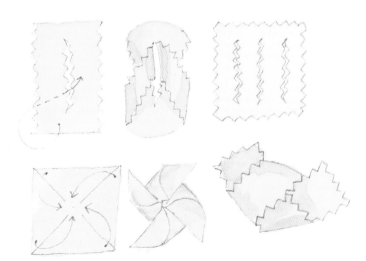

1 Set aside 2 tbsp of flour. Put the rest of the flour on a work surface. Mix in the caster sugar, baking powder and salt. Make a well and put in the butter, egg yolk, grappa and milk. Mix everything together, kneading until the dough is well blended. If it is too hard add a little more milk; if too soft add some of the reserved flour. You can also make the dough in a food processor.

2 Knead the dough for at least 5 minutes as you would with bread or pasta dough. The dough should become smooth and elastic. Make a ball, wrap and leave at room temperature for 1 hour or longer.

3 Roll out the dough <u>very</u> thinly, using either a rolling pin or, better, a hand cranked pasta machine. If you are using the machine, roll through the last notch. The thinness of the dough is the secret of good crostoli.

4 Using a pastry wheel, cut the strips of dough into lasagne-size rectangles. Make 3 parallel slashes in the middle of each rectangle.

5 Heat enough frying oil to come two-thirds of the way up the sides of a frying pan or a wok. When the oil is very hot (a piece of stale bread should take 50 seconds to brown) fry the dough shapes in batches until pale gold and puffy. Lift the crostoli out of the oil with a fish slice and place on kitchen paper towels to drain.

6 Before serving, pile the crostoli on a dish, sprinkling every layer with sifted icing sugar. They are excellent hot or cold.

FRITTELLE DI SEMOLINO
SEMOLINA FRITTERS

These are other Carnival fritters from northern Italy. In my home they were always served with apple fritters and, of course, crostoli (see previous recipe).

1 Bring the milk slowly to the simmer with the granulated sugar, lemon zest, butter and salt, stirring frequently to dissolve the sugar.

2 Add the semolina in a slow stream while beating hard with a wooden spoon to prevent lumps forming. Continue stirring and cooking over low heat for 10 minutes. The mixture will be quite stiff. Draw off the heat and allow to cool for 15 minutes or so. Remove and discard the lemon zest.

3 Mix in the egg yolks, one at a time, beating well to incorporate after each addition.

4 Spread the semolina mixture on a board or flat dish to a thickness of about 2.5cm/1in. Level it down evenly with a damp spatula and leave it to cool completely. You can leave it overnight.

5 Cut the semolina into 2.5cm/1in wide strips and then cut the strips across to make lozenges.

6 Heat oil in a wok or in a deep frying pan to 175°C/330°F – hot enough for a cube of stale bread to brown in 50 seconds.

7 Meanwhile, lightly beat the 2 whole eggs in a bowl and spread the breadcrumbs in a dish. Dip a piece of semolina into the egg and then coat with breadcrumbs, patting them into the semolina.

8 Fry, in 2 or 3 batches, to a lovely gold colour and then put into a dish lined with kitchen paper towels to drain.

9 Serve hot or cold, lavishly sprinkled with sifted icing sugar.

Makes about 24 fritters

1l/1¾pt full fat milk
100g/3½oz granulated sugar
pared strip of unwaxed lemon zest
120g/4oz unsalted butter
pinch of salt
250g/9oz semolina
3 size-2 egg yolks
oil for frying
2 eggs
225g/8oz dried breadcrumbs
icing sugar, to decorate

DOLCI AL CUCCHIAIO

PUDDINGS

I n this section I have collected eight recipes for dolci that are served at dinner parties, some famous, some little known, some elaborate and rich, others simple and modest, but all good and typically Italian.

TIRAMISU

MASCARPONE PUDDING

Serves 6

150ml/¼pt strong espresso coffee
3tbsp brandy
60g/2oz bitter chocolate
2 eggs, at room temperature, separated
1 egg yolk
4 tbsp caster sugar
250g/9oz mascarpone
about 20 Savoiardi biscuits

For the decoration
coffee beans
candied violets (optional)

A book on dolci would hardly be complete without including the most popular of them all, Tiramisù. Surprisingly, considering its popularity, Tiramisù is a relatively new arrival even on the Italian scene. Up to 20 years ago it was only known in the region where it originated, the Veneto.

Savoiardi are available from Italian delicatessens. If you cannot find them, make your own sponge finger biscuits – ordinary sponge fingers or boudoir biscuits from a supermarket will not be absorbent enough.

1 Mix together the coffee and brandy.

2 Grate about one-quarter of the chocolate and cut the rest into small pieces.

3 Beat the 3 egg yolks with the sugar until very pale and softly peaked. Fold the mascarpone in gradually and mix very thoroughly until the mixture is smooth and does not show any lumps.

4 Whisk the 2 egg whites until stiff but not dry and fold gradually into the mascarpone and egg yolk mixture.

5 Dip the biscuits, one at a time, into the coffee and brandy mixture, turning them over once or twice until they become pale brown. Lay 7 biscuits on the bottom of an oval dish, so as to make a base. Spread over one-quarter of the mascarpone cream and scatter with some chocolate pieces. Dip more biscuits into the coffee mixture and make another layer. Spread over one-quarter of the mascarpone cream and scatter with some chocolate pieces. Dip more biscuits into the coffee mixture and make another layer. Spread with another quarter of the cream and scatter with chocolate pieces. Cover with the last layer of moistened biscuits and spread with half the remaining cream.

6 Cover the pudding tightly and put it, with the reserved mascarpone cream, in the fridge to chill for about 6 hours.

7 Before serving, spread the reserved mascarpone cream over the top, smoothing it down neatly with a spatula. Sprinkle the grated chocolate all over the top and decorate with the coffee beans and with the optional candied violets.

CREMA MASCARPONE
MASCARPONE AND RUM CREAM

Similar to the ubiquitous Tiramisù, this dessert is lighter and more subtle. In my family it used to be called 'La Crema del Principe', and it is indeed a royal dessert, smooth and delicate.

The cream can be prepared ahead of time up to step 3. Add the egg whites no longer than 1 hour before serving. Serve with amaretti biscuits, whose dark, almondy flavour is ideal with this dessert.

Serves 4

2 size-2 eggs, separated
2 tbsp caster sugar
2 tbsp dark rum
225g/½lb mascarpone
1 tsp lemon juice
12 amaretti

1 Whisk the egg yolks with the sugar until light and mousse-like, then beat in the rum.

2 Press the mascarpone through a fine sieve and fold into the egg yolk mixture.

3 Whisk the egg whites with the lemon juice until stiff but not dry and fold gently into the mixture until the cream is smooth. Spoon the mixture into long stem glasses and place 1 amaretto on the top. Hand the rest of the amaretti round on a dish. Keep the cream chilled until ready to serve.

LA MERINGA FARCITA
MERINGUE FILLED WITH MARRONS GLACÉS,
CHOCOLATE AND CREAM

Serves 6–8

For the meringue
the whites of 4 size-2 eggs, at
room temperature
1 tsp lemon juice
225g/8 oz caster sugar

For the filling
the whites of 2 size-2 eggs
3 tbsp caster sugar
450ml/¾pt whipping cream
4 tbsp dark rum
225g/½lb marrons glacés, cut
into small pieces
100g/3½oz bitter chocolate, cut
into small pieces
2 tbsp pistachio nuts, blanched,
peeled and chopped
(see page 52)

The meringue in this recipe is Italian meringue, which is more reliable and less fragile than Swiss meringue made with uncooked whites of egg.

1 Heat the oven to 150°C/300°F/Gas Mark 2.

2 Make an Italian meringue as follows. Whisk the egg whites with the lemon juice until stiff. Put the bowl over a saucepan of simmering water and continue whisking while gradually adding the sugar. Whisk until the mixture is warm, silky looking and forming soft peaks.

3 Draw two 20cm/8in circles on siliconised baking parchment. Place the paper on 1 or 2 baking trays. Spoon the meringue over the two circles, smoothing it out with a palette knife. Place the trays in the oven and bake for about 45 minutes or until the meringue is set. Remove the meringue discs from the paper and allow to cool.

4 For the filling, whisk the egg whites in a bowl until stiff. Place the bowl over a saucepan of simmering water and gradually add the sugar, while whisking constantly. When the mixture is warm, remove from the heat and place the base of the bowl in a basin of cold water to cool. This stiff egg white mixture makes the filling lighter, both in texture and in substance.

5 Whip the cream. Fold in the egg white mixture.

6 Add the rum, marrons glacés, chocolate and pistachios and mix well until everything is evenly distributed.

7 Place one of the meringue discs on a flat dish. Spread two-thirds of the filling over it and put the other disc on top. Cover with the remaining filling. Chill for at least 6 hours before serving.

LE DITA DEGLI APOSTOLI
PANCAKES STUFFED WITH RICOTTA

The odd name of this recipe from Puglia, the heel of the Italian boot, means Apostles' Fingers. I can only suppose the pancakes were given this name because their appearance calls to mind long fingers, raised to give a blessing.

This is the recipe developed by my colleague and dear friend Alice Wooledge Salmon from the original recipe by the cookery teacher Paola Pettini, who showed us how to make the Dita during a recent stay in Puglia.

1 To make the pancakes, beat the eggs with the sugar. Mix in the flour and salt and then gradually add the milk while beating constantly. The batter should be fairly liquid. Leave to rest for 1 hour.
2 Meanwhile, prepare the stuffing. Sieve the ricotta into a bowl and fold in the cream and caster sugar. Add all the other ingredients and mix very thoroughly. Chill.
3 Make very thin pancakes in a 28cm/11in pan. (If not using a non-stick pan, grease it lightly with melted butter). You should get 12 large pancakes.
4 Lay the pancakes on the work surface and spread the stuffing thinly all over each one. Roll them up tightly
5 Cut each 'finger' into 3 or 4 pieces, place on a dish and sprinkle with sifted icing sugar. They are traditionally served cold.

Serves 8–10

For the pancakes
5 eggs
30g/1oz caster sugar
120g/4oz plain flour
pinch of salt
250ml/9 fl oz semi-skimmed milk
butter for frying pancakes

For the stuffing
600g/1¼lb fresh ricotta
3 tbsp double cream
250g/9oz caster sugar
grated zest of 1 unwaxed lemon
grated zest of 1 unwaxed orange
grated zest of 1 unwaxed clementine
1½ tbsp finely chopped candied peel
60g/2oz bitter chocolate, cut into small pieces
2 tbsp dark rum
icing sugar, to decorate

MELE ALLE MANDORLE E AL VINO BIANCO

SAUTÉED APPLES WITH ALMONDS
AND WHITE WINE

Serves 6

6 equal-sized large apples such as Granny Smith or other sharp dessert apples
1 unwaxed lemon, scrubbed and washed
60g/2oz unsalted butter
3 cloves
150ml/¼pt Calvados
60g/2oz caster sugar, or more according to the sweetness of the apples
120ml/4fl oz sweet white wine
½ tsp ground cinnamon
90g/3oz flaked almonds
300ml/½pt double cream
4 tbsp icing sugar, sifted

A lovely dessert, this combines the light, fresh flavour of fruit with the richness of a brandy-laced cream.

1 Peel the apples, then cut them in half and remove the cores. Make 6 incisions in the round side of each half, taking care not to cut right through it.

2 Remove the zest from half the lemon using a swivel-action potato peeler, taking care to leave behind the bitter white pith. Squeeze the juice.

3 Heat the butter in a very large sauté pan in which the apple halves will fit comfortably. Add the lemon zest and cloves to the butter and when the butter foam begins to subside, slide in the apples, cut side down. Sauté until golden, then turn the halves over and brown the round side. This will take about 8 minutes. Shake the pan occasionally to prevent the apples sticking.

4 Turn the heat up, pour over one-third of the Calvados and let it bubble away for 30 seconds. Turn the heat down to low and add the caster sugar, wine, lemon juice and 150ml/¼pt of hot water. Cover the pan with the lid or a piece of foil and cook for 5 minutes. Turn the apples over carefully and continue cooking until they are tender. Cooking time varies according to the quality of the apples; do not overcook them or they may break. If necessary add a couple of spoonsful of hot water during the cooking.

5 When the apples are ready – test them by piercing them with the blade of a small knife through their thickest part – transfer them gently to a dish using a slotted spoon. Leave to cool.

6 Remove the lemon zest and cloves from the pan. Add the cinnamon and almonds and sauté over moderate heat for 5 minutes, stirring constantly, until the syrup is thick and the almonds are caramelized. Draw off the heat.

7 Whip the cream. Add the remaining Calvados and the icing sugar and whip again. Spread the cream over a shallow serving dish. Make 12 hollows in the cream with the back of a spoon and lay the apple halves in the hollows, cut side up. Spoon the syrup-coated almonds over the apples. Serve at room temperature.

FRUTTA COTTA AL FORNO
COMPÔTE OF MIXED FRUIT

T he simplicity of this pudding should not deter you from trying it. The fruit, well cooked yet still in neat pieces, absorbs the flavour of the wine that, through the long cooking, has lost the taste of alcohol, which can be unpleasant when cooked with food. Buy prunes that don't need to be soaked.

Serves 4

1 pear, Comice or William's
2 apples, Cox's or Granny Smith
1 banana
2 oranges
6 pitted prunes
grated zest of 1 small lemon
3 tbsp sugar
120ml/4fl oz robust red wine,
such as Barbera

1 Heat the oven to 180°C/350°F/Gas Mark 4.

2 Peel and core the pear and apples. Peel the banana and oranges. Slice them all quite thinly, keeping them separate.

3 Lay the sliced fruit in layers in a 1l/2pt oven dish, arranging it so that each fruit is topped with a different fruit. Scatter the prunes here and there and sprinkle with the lemon zest and sugar. Pour over the wine and cover the dish. Bake for 30 minutes.

4 Uncover the dish and press the fruit down with a slotted spoon to release more liquid. Bake for a further 15 minutes. Serve warm, with or without cream.

ZUCCOTTO

FLORENTINE CREAM PUDDING

Serves 8–10

75g/2½oz almonds, blanched
and peeled (see page 28)
75g/2½oz hazelnuts
3 tbsp brandy
3 tbsp Amaretto
3 tbsp Maraschino or other
sweet liqueur
250g/9oz Madeira cake, cut
into 5mm/¼in thick slices
150g/5oz bitter chocolate
450ml/¾pt whipping cream
90g/3oz icing sugar, sifted

For the decoration

2 tbsp icing sugar
1 tbsp cocoa powder, sifted

A rich creamy pudding from Florence. Its domed shape is like half a pumpkin (*zucca* in Italian) and it is decorated with alternate brown and white segments, like the cupola of Florence cathedral.

1 Heat the oven to 200°C/400°F/Gas Mark 6. Put the almonds and hazelnuts on separate baking trays and toast in the oven for 5 minutes. Then, with a rough towel, rub off as much of the hazelnut skins as you can. Roughly chop the almonds and hazelnuts and set aside.

2 Mix the three liqueurs together. Line the inside of a 1.5l/2½pt pudding basin with cling film and then with cake slices, reserving some for the top. Moisten the cake with most of the liqueur mixture.

3 Melt 60g/2oz of the chocolate in a small bowl set over a pan of simmering water; set aside. Cut the remaining chocolate into small pieces.

4 Whip the cream with the icing sugar until stiff. Fold in the almonds, hazelnuts and chocolate pieces.

5 Divide the cream mixture in half and spoon one portion into the mould, spreading it evenly all over the cake lining the bottom and sides. Fold the melted chocolate into the remaining cream mixture and spoon it into the mould to fill the cavity. Cover the pudding with the reserved cake and moisten it with the rest of the liqueur. Cover the mould with cling film and refrigerate for at least 12 hours.

6 To unmould, place a piece of greaseproof paper and then a piece of cardboard over the top of the pudding basin. Turn the basin over to turn out the pudding on to the paper and cardboard.

Place on a board, remove the basin and peel off the cling film.

7 To decorate the pudding, cut out a circle of greaseproof paper 37cm/15in in diameter. Fold in two to make a half moon, then fold this in two to make a triangle. Fold the triangle in two again to make a thinner triangle. Open out and cut out each alternate section, without cutting the paper through at the top.

8 Dust the whole dome with some sifted icing sugar. Mix 2 tbsp of sifted icing sugar with the cocoa. Place the cut-out circle of paper over the dome and sprinkle the cocoa and sugar mixture in the cut-out sections. Remove the paper carefully without spoiling the pattern. Transfer the pudding to a flat round serving dish, using the cardboard for support. Serve chilled.

ZUPPA INGLESE

CAKE AND CUSTARD PUDDING

Serves 6

150ml/¼pt double cream
350g/¾lb best Madeira cake, cut into 5mm/¼in slices
4 tbsp rum
4 tbsp cherry brandy
2 egg whites, at room temperature
5 tbsp icing sugar, sifted
1 tbsp caster sugar

For the custard
500ml/18fl oz full fat milk
2 strips of lemon zest
3 egg yolks
75g/2½oz caster sugar
50g/1¾oz plain flour

Zuppa Inglese used to be on almost every menu in restaurants within Italy and elsewhere, just as Tiramisù is today. And, like Tiramisù, it can be delicious or a disaster. It all depends on the light balance of the ingredients used.

The name Zuppa Inglese – English soup – is a mystery. Like other Italian writers on the subject, I think the pudding must owe its origin to English trifle, which would have been brought to Tuscany and Naples by the English in the eighteenth and nineteenth centuries.

The liqueur Alchermes, used in Italy, is hardly available elsewhere. Cherry brandy is a good substitute.

1 First make the custard. Bring the milk to the boil with the lemon zest and set aside.
2 Beat the egg yolks with the sugar until pale yellow and light. Beat the flour into the mixture and then slowly pour in the hot milk.
3 Transfer the custard to a heavy-bottomed saucepan and place over very low heat. Cook, stirring the whole time, until the custard becomes very thick and an occasional bubble breaks through the surface. Simmer very gently for a couple of minutes longer. Place the base of the saucepan in a bowl of iced water to cool the custard quickly. Stir frequently.
4 Whip the cream until soft peaks form. When the custard is cold, fold in the cream.
5 Choose a soufflé dish of 1.75l/2¾pt capacity and line it with greaseproof paper or siliconised baking parchment, which will help in unmoulding the pudding.

6 Line the bottom of the soufflé dish with slices of cake, plugging any holes with pieces of cake. Sprinkle with some rum and spread a couple of spoonsful of custard over the cake.

7 Cover with another layer of cake, moisten it with cherry brandy and then spread over some custard. Repeat these layers, ending with the cake moistened with one of the liqueurs.

8 Cover the pudding with cling film, place it in the refrigerator and chill for at least 8 hours, or better still 24 hours, to allow all the flavours to combine.

9 Some 6 hours before you want to serve the pudding, heat the oven to 110°C/225°F/Gas Mark $\frac{1}{4}$. Whisk the egg whites with the icing sugar until stiff. Remove the pudding from the refrigerator and turn it out on to a round serving dish that can be put in the oven at a low temperature. Spread the meringue all over the pudding and sprinkle with the caster sugar. Bake until the meringue is dry and very pale blond in colour, about $\frac{1}{4}$ hour to 20 minutes. Allow to cool and then replace the pudding in the refrigerator to chill for at least 2 hours before serving.

GELATI, SORBETTI E GELATINE

ICE-CREAMS, SORBETS AND FRUIT JELLIES

I could write a whole book on these sweets, so choosing just a few recipes was quite difficult. Gelati and sorbetti had their origins in Italy, and it was the Italian emigrants who took them to the USA, where people have now adopted them and made them their own.

I find that only in Italy can you still find excellent ices in specialist *gelaterie* – ice-cream shops where the ice-creams are made on the premises. The choice is bewildering. Some new favourite flavours, such as tiramisù and zuppa inglese, compete with the lovely old classics, gelato al caffè or al limone. The fruit water-ices are the best because of the strong flavour of the fruit, ripened in the hot sun.

Fruit jellies are now making a welcome come-back on the tables of health-conscious people, and I have included two recipes for them at the end of this section.

SPUMONE AL CIOCCOLATO

FROZEN CHOCOLATE CREAM LOAF

Serves 8

150g/5oz bitter chocolate
350ml/12fl oz full fat milk
4 egg yolks
120g/4oz sugar
4 level tsp plain flour
4 tbsp strong espresso coffee
300ml/½pt whipping cream,
very cold
12 amaretti (optional)
120ml/4fl oz Marsala or
medium sherry (optional)

A *spumone* is a kind of soft ice-cream. Spumoni are always moulded in a tin, usually a loaf tin, and served cut into slices like a pâté. This is the recipe for a chocolate spumone of a delicate creamy flavour. You need best quality chocolate with a high cocoa butter content.

This spumone is particularly delicious covered with amaretti that have been lightly soaked in Marsala or sherry.

1 Melt the chocolate in a bain-marie.

2 Heat the milk to simmering point.

3 Meanwhile, beat the egg yolks with the sugar until pale and light. Add the flour and beat well. Slowly pour over the hot milk, while beating constantly. Transfer the custard to a heavy-bottomed saucepan and cook over the lowest heat, stirring constantly, until the custard thickens and some bubbles break on the surface. Cook for a couple of minutes longer, never ceasing to stir.

4 Mix the melted chocolate and the coffee into the custard. Put the base of the saucepan in a basin of cold water to cool the custard quickly. Stir every now and then.

5 Whip the cream. When the custard is cold, fold in the cream.

6 Line a 1.5l/2½pt loaf tin with foil or greaseproof paper. Spoon the mixture into the tin and freeze overnight.

7 Remove from the freezer 1 hour before serving. Unmould on to a rectangular dish and cut into slices to serve.

Note: If you wish to cover the ice-cream with amaretti, briefly dip the biscuits in the Marsala or sherry and lay them over the spumone just before serving.

SEMIFREDDO DI ZABAGLIONE AL CAFFE
FROZEN COFFEE ZABAGLIONE

A 'semifreddo' cannot be frozen hard because of the high sugar content in the meringue. This why it is called 'half-cold', and why its consistency is so soft and voluptuous.

1 In the upper part of a double boiler or in a heatproof bowl, beat the 5 egg yolks with the caster sugar until pale and forming ribbons. Add the cinnamon and Marsala or sherry and continue beating for a minute or so.

2 Put some water in the lower part of the double boiler or in a saucepan in which the bowl can be placed. Turn the heat on and put in place the top of the double boiler or the bowl containing the egg yolk mixture. Beat the mixture constantly while it heats, until it becomes a soft foamy mass. Remove from the heat and add the coffee. Place in a sink of cold water to cool. Stir the zabaglione every now and then to prevent a skin forming.

3 Whip the cream and fold into the zabaglione lightly but thoroughly.

4 Whisk the egg whites until firm. Gradually add the icing sugar and continue beating until the meringue forms stiff peaks. Fold it 1 or 2 spoonfuls at a time into the egg yolk mixture.

5 Spoon the zabaglione into a glass bowl or individual glasses and freeze overnight.

6 Decorate with coffee beans and blobs of whipped cream before serving.

Serves 6

3 eggs, separated
2 egg yolks
120g/4oz caster sugar
pinch of ground cinnamon
150ml/¼pt Marsala or medium sweet sherry
4 tbsp strong espresso coffee
225ml/8fl oz whipping cream
100g/3½oz icing sugar, sifted
coffee beans and whipped cream, for decoration

SORBETTO AL MANDARINO

CLEMENTINE SORBET

Serves 4

180g/6oz sugar
pared zest of 1 unwaxed lemon,
without any white pith
pared zest of 1 unwaxed orange,
without any white pith
300ml/½pt freshly squeezed
clementine juice
4tbsp freshly squeezed orange
juice
4 tbsp freshly squeezed lemon
juice
2 tbsp white rum

Unfortunately, tasty mandarin oranges are a fruit of the past. However, the tasteless satsumas seem at last to have given way to the new hybrid, clementines, which have recaptured some of the flavour of the mandarin.

This sorbet can also be made with fresh orange juice to which the juice of a lemon is added.

1 Put the sugar, lemon and orange zest and 300ml/½pt of water in a heavy-bottomed saucepan. Bring slowly to the boil and simmer for 5 minutes. Allow to cool, then strain the syrup.
2 Strain the fruit juices and add to the cold syrup with the rum. Mix well and pour the mixture into an ice-cream machine. Freeze according to the manufacturer's instructions.

CASSATA GELATA

ICED CASSATA

Serves 6–8

600ml/1pt full fat milk
grated zest of 1 unwaxed lemon
5 egg yolks
150g/5oz caster sugar
30g/1oz almonds
30g/1oz pistachio nuts
150ml/¼pt whipping cream
30g/1oz candied fruit or
candied peel, chopped
1 tbsp icing sugar, sifted

This is the original, home-made, recipe for the cassata that is now sold frozen in supermarkets. It is quite a lengthy dish to make but it is easy, even if you do not have an ice-cream machine.

You can substitute bits of best chocolate for the pistachio nuts.

1 Heat the milk to simmering point with the lemon zest.
2 Put the egg yolks and caster sugar in a bowl (metal if possible as this will transmit heat and cold more quickly) and beat until pale and mousse-like. I use a hand-held electric beater. Then

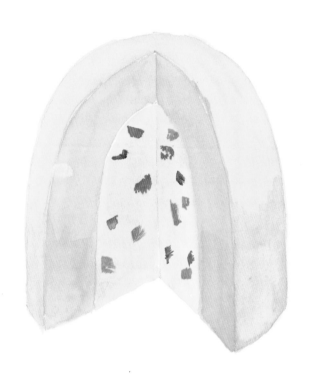

place the bowl over a saucepan of gently simmering water. Add the hot milk while whisking the whole time. Cook until the custard thickens and will coat the back of a spoon. This can easily take as long as 25 minutes. Stir constantly and do not allow the custard to boil or the egg will curdle.

3 As soon as the custard is ready, draw from the heat and set the base of the bowl in a basin of cold water. Allow to cool, stirring frequently. When the custard is cold, strain it to remove the lemon zest, then freeze in an ice-cream machine following the manufacturer's instructions, or still-freeze in the freezer. Do not freeze hard.

4 Place a 1.2l/2pt bombe mould (or a metal mould and a piece of foil to act as a lid) in the freezer to chill for 30 minutes.

5 Spoon the custard ice-cream into the chilled mould, lining the bottom and sides evenly but leaving a hole in the middle. Return the mould to the freezer.

6 Blanch the almonds in boiling water for 30 seconds and then squeeze them in your fingers to remove the skins. Dry and chop them coarsely. Do the same with the pistachio nuts.

7 Whip the cream and fold in the almonds, pistachios, candied fruit, and icing sugar. Spoon this mixture into the centre of the ice-cream lined mould and return it to the freezer. Freeze for at least 4 hours.

8 About an hour before serving, remove the lid from the mould, cover the mould with a flat dish and turn them over. Put the mould, on the dish, in the fridge. By the time you wish to serve the cassata you should be able to lift the mould off easily. If the cassata is still frozen on to the mould, dip the mould quickly into very hot water for a few seconds.

GELATINE DI FRUTTA

The image of fruit jellies has been debased by the synthetic-tasting jellies made from packets of jelly powder dissolved in water. In Italy these do not exist; the Italians have always made their jellies from the juice of the fresh fruit. These jellies were particularly popular in the Renaissance, when they were made in various shapes and guises to become the centrepieces of lavishly adorned tables.

Here are two fruit jellies, one for the summer and one for the winter. I use leaf gelatine, not gelatine powder, because it does not have the unpleasant gluey flavour of the powder, and because it dissolves more evenly. Leaf gelatine is sold in the best super-markets and delicatessens.

GELATINA DI ARANCIA
ORANGE JELLY

Serves 4 to 6

20g/¾oz leaf gelatine
150g/5oz sugar
300ml/½pt freshly squeezed
orange juice, strained
4 tbsp freshly squeezed lemon
juice, strained
2 tbsp Grand Marnier
4 tbsp white rum

Buy oranges with full flavour and the right amount of acidity. I use only Italian or Spanish oranges, which have these highly important attributes.

1 Soak the gelatine leaves in cold water for at least 30 minutes.
2 Put the sugar and the strained fruit juices in a saucepan. Bring very slowly to the boil and simmer until the sugar has dissolved, stirring occasionally. Draw off the heat.
3 Put 200ml/7fl oz of water in a saucepan. Lift the gelatine leaves out of the soaking water and squeeze out the liquid. Add to the pan of water and heat gently until the gelatine has dissolved, beating constantly with a small wire balloon whisk. Pour into the fruit syrup and add the two liqueurs. Stir very thoroughly and allow to cool.

4 Grease a 750ml/1¼pt jelly mould with a non-tasting vegetable oil or with almond oil. Pour the mixture into the mould and chill overnight or for at least 6 hours.

5 To turn out, immerse the mould for a few seconds in a basin of warm water. Place a flat dish over the mould and turn the whole thing upside down. Pat the mould and give a few jerks to the dish. the jelly should now turn out easily. Put the mould back on the jelly to cover it and replace the dish in the fridge until ready to serve.

I like to serve this orange jelly with sliced oranges topped with passion fruit. For 4 people you will need 4–5 oranges, 2 tbsp caster sugar and 3 passion fruits. Peel the oranges to the quick and slice very thinly. Put them in a bowl and gently mix in the sugar. Cut the passion fruits in half and with a pointed coffee spoon scoop out the little green seeds and the juice, spreading them all over the orange slices. Make the dish at least 2 hours in advance and keep it refrigerated, covered with cling film.

GELATINA DI MORE O DI RIBES

—— BLACKBERRY OR REDCURRANT JELLY ——

Serves 4–5

20g/¾oz leaf gelatine
120g/4oz sugar
piece of vanilla pod, 5cm/2in
long
300ml/½pt pure blackberry or
redcurrant juice
4 tbsp Marsala
juice of ½ lemon
150ml/¼pt whipping cream

This is a thick jelly, rich in colour and flavour, suitable for serving in individual bowls. I suggest you make your own fruit juice by boiling the fruit for 2–3 minutes and then straining it through a sieve lined with muslin.

1 Soak the gelatine leaves in cold water for at least 30 minutes.
2 Put the sugar, 100ml/3½fl oz of water and the vanilla pod in a small saucepan. Bring slowly to the boil, stirring frequently. Simmer for 10 minutes.
3 Squeeze the water out of the gelatine leaves. Add the gelatine to the sugar syrup and allow it to dissolve, while whisking constantly.
4 When the gelatine is thoroughly dissolved draw the pan off the heat. Remove and discard the vanilla pod. Add the fruit juice, Marsala and lemon juice and mix very thoroughly.
5 Spoon the fruit syrup into 4 or 5 bowls. Chill in the refrigerator for at least 6 hours.
6 Whip the cream and drop a spoonful on top of each bowl. Return to the fridge until you are ready to serve the jelly.

LIST OF RECIPES